Want to Know Your Idol?

KT-434-311

OLLY Murs

BY KAY BARNHAM

000000791025

WAYLAND

First published in 2013 by Wayland
Copyright © Wayland 2013

Wayland
338 Euston Road
London NW1 3BH

Wayland Australia
Level 17/207 Kent Street
Sydney, NSW 2000

DUDLEY PUBLIC LIBRARIES	
000000791025	
£5.99	920 MUR
09-Jan-2014	PETERS

All rights reserved

Commissioning editor: Debbie Foy
Designer: Ray Bryant
Series editor: Camilla Lloyd

Dewey ref: 782.4'2164'092-dc23
ISBN: 978 0 7502 7836 2
10 9 8 7 6 5 4 3 2 1

Printed in UK
Wayland is a division of Hachette Children's Books,
an Hachette UK company

www.hachette.co.uk

The author and publisher would like to thank the following for allowing
their pictures to be reproduced in this publication: Cover and 47 © LDR/
Splash News/Corbis; 4 © PHIL PENMAN/Splash News/Corbis; 19 © Chris
Schwegler/Retna Ltd./Corbis; 33 © KHAP/Splash News/Corbis; 37 © Splash
News/Corbis; 39 © Splash News/Corbis; 41 © Comic Relief/ /Splash News/
Corbis; 59 © KHAP/Splash News/Corbis; 67 © 247PapsTV/ /Splash News/
Corbis; 89 © PHIL PENMAN/Splash News/Corbis.

This book is not affiliated with or endorsed by Olly Murs or any of
his publishers or licensees.

Olly Murs is a registered trademark of OLIVER MURS.

Want to know
EVERYTHING
there is to
know about

OLLY
MURS?

Then head this way...

He's probably the nicest, friendliest, **CHEERIEST POP STAR** you'll ever meet. And the world's best advert for funky hats. But it's the fact that he's a total **SINGING SENSATION** that has propelled this talented chap from an everyday job in a call centre to the biggest venues in the world and **TOTAL** superstardom.

Who is he?

Olly Murs,
of course!

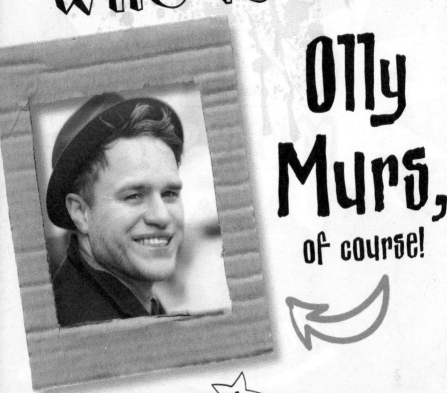

If you're reading this, then you're probably already an **Olly Murs** fan. But how much of a fan are you? Do you know everything there is to know about your idol? Do you know what colour his eyes are? What's the name of that hat he usually he wears? What does he really think of **Robbie Williams**? And is it true that he fired a member of **JLS** out of a cannon?

This book tells you **everything** you need to know about Olly Murs. Right now, you're just a few pages away from becoming one of his biggest fans EVER. But there's more. Armed with your new stack of facts, you'll also get to prove your **über-fan status** by scoring top marks in the fiendishly difficult quizzes dotted throughout the book.

WANT TO KNOW
YOUR IDOL?

All you have to do
is turn the page...

OLIVER STANLEY MURS WAS BORN
IN WITHAM, ESSEX, UK ON
14 MAY 1984, WHICH WAS **EXACTLY**
THE SAME DAY AS HIS BROTHER, BEN.

Coincidence?

ERR, NO.
THEY'RE **TWINS**.

At first, Olly's life was nothing
out of the ordinary. He didn't go
to stage school. He didn't wow
talent scouts in a lead role in
the school musical. He certainly
wasn't a star. But he had a dream.
He wanted to be a ...

FOOTBALLER!

It's totally true.

OLLY **LOVES** FOOTBALL. DID YOU KNOW THAT HE'S ALWAYS BEEN ONE OF MANCHESTER UNITED'S BIGGEST FANS?

You do now. But what you may **NOT** know is that Olly is actually quite a good **football player** himself. He was the striker for his school football team, then played for Witham Town FC, too. It was surely only a matter of time before he ended up in a championship league team and became...

FAMOUS?

But then ...
disaster struck!

AND IN THE STYLE OF TV DRAMAS THAT MAKE YOU WAIT UNTIL NEXT WEEK TO DISCOVER WHAT HAPPENED NEXT, YOU'LL JUST HAVE TO TURN TO PAGES 14-15 TO FIND OUT MORE.

'I get involved in everything I do musically. It's an important part of what I do and it's something I'm very proud of. I want the music to feel like it's my music, typical of my personality.'

Olly Murs

OLLY MURS' FACEBOOK PAGE HAS OVER **THREE MILLION** 'LIKES'.

(That's more than the population of Chicago, USA!)

BUT IF YOU THINK THAT'S IMPRESSIVE, THEN CHECK OUT HOW MANY FANS FOLLOW HIM ON TWITTER... IT'S OVER...

...FOUR AND A HALF MILLION!

(And that is more than the entire population of Los Angeles, USA!)

 What a popular lad!

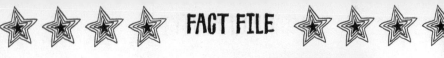

Olly Murs

FULL NAME: Oliver Stanley Murs

DATE OF BIRTH: 14 May 1984

PLACE OF BIRTH: Witham, Essex, UK

HEIGHT: 175cm (5 feet 9 inches)

EYE COLOUR: Brown

HAIR COLOUR: Brown

FAVOURITE COLOUR: Blue

FAVOURITE CLOTHES: Jeans, Shirt, Waistcoat and Funky Hat

TWITTER NAME: @OLLYOFFICIAL

DAD

Peter Murs, whose family comes from Latvia, works as a toolmaker in Chelmsford, Essex. Pete is a very **proud dad**.

MUM

Vicky-Lynn Murs likes to help out her famous son whenever she can. She's supported him throughout his singing career and even waded in to help when **traffic jams** meant that people missed seeing Olly in concert, personally emailing upset fans. How **FAB**.

TWIN BROTHER

Ben Murs is just a tiny bit younger than Olly, but obviously they share a birthday. Sadly, the pair fell out when Olly couldn't go to Ben's wedding because it clashed with **The X Factor** rehearsals. But hopefully they'll make up one day...

SISTER

Olly's sister is called Fay and although her brother's now **so famous** that she doesn't get to spend much time with him – except at Christmas, of course – she's VERY proud of him.

FAVOURITES

THESE ARE SOME OF OLLY'S
MOST FAVOURITE THINGS
IN THE WORLD:

Biscuit:
Custard creams

Sweet:
Sherbert dibdab,
but he'll settle for
sherbert fountains

Food:
His mum's
roast dinner

Pudding:
Cheesecake or
ice cream

Fruit:
Banana

Song:
Billie Jean by
Michael Jackson

Singer:
Michael Jackson

Football Club:
Manchester United

TV mathematician:
Carol Vorderman

Dog:
French bulldog

Type of dancing:
Robotic

Actress:
Mila Kunis

**Female
X Factor judges:**
Dannii Minogue
and Cheryl Cole

Movies:
The Goonies and
Ghostbusters

12

Olly loves music so much that if he could only take one thing to a **desert island**, it would be a gadget on which to play his **favourite tracks**. (Though a box of matches and a tent might be more useful, Olly.)

He once spent a day being an **agony uncle** for a girls' magazine, dispensing lots of good advice to readers who had written in with their problems. **Awww**. What a lovely boy.

He loves listening to **indie rock** music.

He's a terrible cook. **Beans on toast** with cheese on top is the only thing he can make.

DISASTER!

THE WORST THING THAT CAN POSSIBLY HAPPEN TO A WANNABE FOOTBALLER HAPPENED TO OLLY MURS.

He was injured on the pitch. After damaging a ligament in his left knee, he had to have keyhole surgery. Afterwards, the bad news was that poor Olly had to give up on his dream of being a top footballer.

Oh noooo.

It was back to real life for Olly, who got a job in telesales and instead of training at the **football ground**, spent his spare time going out with his mates. Luckily it didn't take much effort for his friends to convince him to sing along with the local **karaoke machine**. And they soon realised that he was really rather good. Which was lucky, because, guess what? Deep down - even deeper than the dream Olly had of being a footballer - he had another dream.

Olly Murs wanted to be a ...

POPSTAR!

Yay!

So he auditioned for **The X Factor** in 2007.

He didn't get through.

He tried again in 2008.

He still didn't get through.

But in a display of surely what is the best ever example of **pop perseverance**, in 2009, at the age of 23, Olly Murs reapplied for **The X Factor** and finally...

HE GOT THROUGH.

Aren't you glad he didn't give up?

OLLY MURS WAS BORN ON 14 MAY 1984, WHICH MAKES HIM A TAURUS. ACCORDING TO ASTROLOGERS, THIS MEANS THAT HE IS

patient, loving, determined and calm.

(How lovely!)

BUT HE IS ALSO

jealous, resentful and greedy...

(Oh dear.)

16

TAUREANS ARE MOST LIKELY TO GET ON
WITH THOSE BORN UNDER THE STAR
SIGNS OF CAPRICORN AND VIRGO.
BUT HE'LL ALSO GET ON WITH

cancer, Gemini,
Pisces and Aries.

Are YOU one of the lucky few...?

Bonus
birthday
fact!

Not only was Olly born on the same day
as his twin brother Ben, he was also born
on the same day as Facebook supremo
Mark Zuckerberg! And all three of them
share a birthday with actresses **Miranda
Cosgrove** and **Cate Blanchett** and Star
Wars director **George Lucas**.

'It wasn't like I was auditioning or doing loads of shows for years and years – I wasn't. I'd get up and do a bit of **karaoke** and a bit of singing here and there, but no one was ever thinking there was an **opportunity** for me to be a pop star. I just decided one day, completely out of the blue, "I'll do **The X Factor** and see what happens".'

Olly Murs

'OLLY MURS IS SO TOTALLY CUTE. I CAN'T WAIT TO SEE HIM IN CONCERT. I LIKE HIS SONGS BECAUSE THEY ARE REALLY HAPPY AND I CAN'T STOP LISTENING TO THEM... ESPECIALLY **HEART SKIPS A BEAT** AND **TROUBLEMAKER**.'

Maya, 12

Which of these tracks HASN'T Olly released?

Please don't let me go

Don't leave me this way

Dance with me tonight

Heart of glass

Army of two

Thinking of me

Oliver's Army

Heart skips a beat

Dancing Queen

Troublemaker

Trouble

Do you think of me

All answers on pages 90-93

21

BEFORE **THE X FACTOR** BLASTED HIM TO POP SUPERSTARDOM, OLLY MURS HAD NEVER HAD A SINGING LESSON IN HIS LIFE. BUT HE WASN'T DETERRED FROM ENTERING THE TV TALENT SHOW.

 ## Not a bit of it.

During the sixth series of **The X Factor** in 2009, Olly repeatedly wowed the judges with his versions of these songs:

SUPERSTITION

SHE'S THE ONE

A FOOL IN LOVE

BEWITCHED

COME TOGETHER

TWIST AND SHOUT

DON'T STOP ME NOW

FASTLOVE

CAN YOU FEEL IT

WE CAN WORK IT OUT

ANGELS (DUET WITH ROBBIE WILLIAM)

BUT AFTER BRILLIANT FEEDBACK
FROM THE JUDGES AND HUGE PUBLIC
SUPPORT, THERE WAS A HUGE SHOCKER
IN THE FINAL THAT THREATENED TO
RUIN OLLY'S DREAM FOR EVER...

Joe McElderry won.

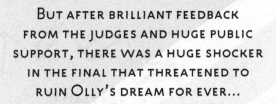

NOOOOOOOOOOOOO!

But all wasn't lost. Two loooong
days later, Olly's **army of fans**
were rewarded with the best
news ever: Olly Murs was going to
be offered a record deal with none
other than **Simon Cowell** himself.

YES!

Olly Murs was going to hit the big time after all!

'...THE EASIEST YES I'VE EVER GIVEN...'

SIMON COWELL, AFTER LISTENING TO OLLY SING **SUPERSTITION** IN HIS FIRST AUDITION.

'...IN A DIFFERENT LEAGUE...'

SIMON COWELL, AFTER OLLY SANG **A FOOL IN LOVE** ON **THE X FACTOR**.

'...THE DARK HORSE OF THE COMPETITION...'

LOUIS WALSH, AFTER OLLY HAD SUNG **BEWITCHED** IN WEEK THREE OF THE COMPETITION.

'...THE BEST RISK I HAVE EVER TAKEN IN MY LIFE...'

SIMON COWELL, DURING THE X FACTOR FINAL.

'...ABSOLUTELY THE BEST PERFORMER WE HAVE ON THE SHOW BY FAR ...'

DANNII MINOGUE, AFTER SINGING DON'T STOP ME NOW IN WEEK SIX.

'YOU ABSOLUTELY TORE [THAT SONG] FROM YOUR SOUL. I'VE NEVER HEARD YOU SING LIKE THAT.'

CHERYL COLE, AFTER OLLY SANG THE CLIMB IN THE X FACTOR FINAL.

'YOU'RE A BORN, BORN SHOWMAN AND NO MATTER WHAT HAPPENS TONIGHT YOU'RE GOING TO HAVE A GREAT CAREER IN MUSIC.'

LOUIS WALSH, DURING THE X FACTOR FINAL.

FAN-TASTIC!

OLLY MURS HAS LOADS OF FANS –
OVER 4 MILLION OF THEM ON TWITTER
ALONE – AND THEY **LOVE** THEIR IDOL.

Here are just a few of Olly's most devoted fans:

• Perhaps Olly's most famous fan ever was the one who wrapped herself in Christmas wrapping paper and posted herself to **The X Factor** House. She didn't make it inside, but she did get Olly's autograph.

• When one fan turned up outside a Dublin radio station, she didn't ask Olly to sign an **autograph book** or a scrap of paper. She asked him to sign HER instead. So he did. (Even though he looked a little bemused.)

• One young fan queued for six hours to meet her idol at a **book signing** in Glasgow. But when she DID reach the front of the queue, it was all too much and she burst into **FLOODS** of tears. Lovely Olly cheered the über-fan up by having his photo taken with her.

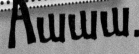

HERE ARE JUST A FEW OF THE
WEIRD AND WONDERFUL (AND VERY
ORDINARY) PRESENTS THAT **OLLY'S**
MANY FANS HAVE GIVEN HIM SO FAR...

- Sherbert
(his favourite type of sweet)

- A mug
(with actual tea in it)

- A mug
(with the fan's face printed on it)

- Bottles and bottles
and bottles of cologne
(after he admitted
to being a big fan of
the smelly stuff - he's
probably got enough
now, thanks)

Unscramble the letters to find the fabulous tracks that Olly has sung so far.

1. A GELLED POSTMEN TOE

2. HABITAT SPEAKERS

3. CANTEEN DO WITH MIGHT

4. BLAME OUR TREK

5. ROOMY WAFT

6. FINE KING MOTH

Now, FOR BONUS POINTS AND A ROUND OF **OLLY MURS** APPLAUSE, MATCH THE DECODED SONG TITLES WITH THE ALBUMS ON WHICH THEY FEATURE!

OLLY MURS

IN CASE YOU DIDN'T KNOW

RIGHT PLACE RIGHT TIME

All answers on pages 90-93

When Olly Murs appeared on Channel 4's **Stand Up To Cancer** in aid of Cancer Research, he didn't expect it to go with quite so much of a bang...

The programme makers needed someone to volunteer to be shot out of a cannon, so **JLS singer Aston Merrygold** stepped forward...

Bravo!

So far, so good.

Then they needed someone to press the button to fire the **human cannonball**. Olly was chosen to do it.

Excellent.

And then everything seemed to go **SPECTACULARLY** wrong...

Olly pressed the button and nothing happened. So he jabbed it again harder this time. But it looked as if the firing mechanism wasn't working properly because although the cannon boomed and Aston was launched into the air, he didn't land on the safety mat but instead went soaring way over it, landing in a crumpled heap on the floor beyond.

GASP!

There was mayhem. Paramedics rushed to the motionless popstar's aid. And for two whole minutes things looked really bad.

POOR OLLY WAS **HORRIFIED**. WAS IT HIS FAULT? HAD HE KILLED ONE OF JLS?

And THEN **'Aston'** was revealed to be a (totally unharmed) **stuntman** and the real Aston Merrygold (also totally unharmed, because he hadn't gone anywhere near the cannon) stepped forward.

IT WAS ALL A PRACTICAL JOKE.

PHEW!

'...[Olly Murs'] songs are perhaps the purest expression of pop right now: they are happy, catchy, and full of a boundless and thoroughly unpretentious enthusiasm it's difficult to resist.'

Nick Duerden, The Independent.

'Taking its cue from latter-day Take That and underpinned by military drumming, **Army of Two** is a pop thumper of the highest order.'

John Aizlewood's review of Olly Murs' Right Place, Right Time **album, on** BBC Music.

'he's a pleasantly breezy pop-ska singer, and it would have been a hard soul who didn't jiggle a bit to a finale of **Heart Skips a Beat**.'

Caroline Sullivan, The Guardian, **reviewing an Olly Murs 2012 concert.**

'...**One Of These Days** is a great piano ballad; **Troublemaker** a brutally efficient disco-funk track; while **Head To Toe** is a rumbling boogie that wouldn't have shamed The Jackson 5.'

John Lewis, Metro, **reviewing Olly's** Right Place, Right Time **album.**

by @ollyofficial

Gunna find it hard to move on stage tonight... In **MANCHESTAAAAAAR!!** Legs are like rocks!!

Arrived back... **JUST!** Highlight of the night is me, dazza, jon getting changed at baggage reclaim. Good job I've done quick changes on tour lol

OH MY DAYS!! 4 MILLION twitter followers.. Not sure what to say but just cheers!! Hope I keep things interesting!! Lot of pressure now haha

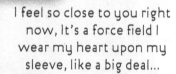

I feel so close to you right now, It's a force field I wear my heart upon my sleeve, like a big deal...

OLLY MURS ISN'T THE ONLY
CELEBRITY TO COME FROM ESSEX.
OTHER FAMOUS NEIGHBOURS,
PAST AND PRESENT, INCLUDE...

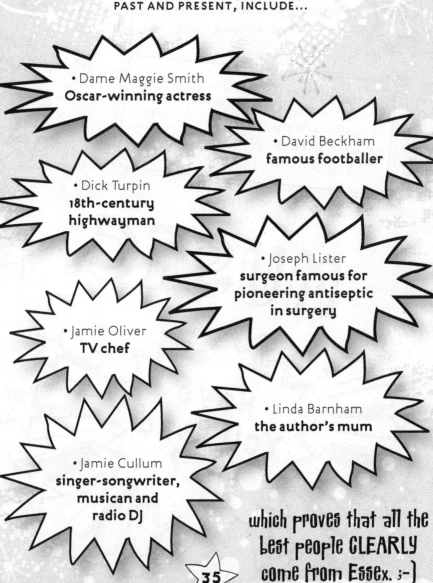

• Dame Maggie Smith
Oscar-winning actress

• David Beckham
famous footballer

• Dick Turpin
**18th-century
highwayman**

• Joseph Lister
**surgeon famous for
pioneering antiseptic
in surgery**

• Jamie Oliver
TV chef

• Linda Barnham
the author's mum

• Jamie Cullum
**singer-songwriter,
musican and
radio DJ**

which proves that all the
best people CLEARLY
come from Essex. ;-)

OLLY MURS ALWAYS SEEMS SUCH A CHEERY CHAP THAT HE LOOKS AS IF HE MUST HAVE PLENTY OF HAPPY DAYS. SO WHEN HIS AUTOBIOGRAPHY WAS PUBLISHED, THAT'S EXACTLY WHAT HE CALLED IT!

Happy Days (Coronet, 2012) is the story of Olly's rise to fame and the emotional highs and lows on the way. But more than anything else, it's about the subject that's closest to his heart:

MUSIC.

Have you read it...?

OLLY MURS HAS RAISED BUCKETS OF CASH FOR CHARITY BY BEING PART OF THE GROUP THAT TREKKED THROUGH KENYA IN 2011 FOR **RED NOSE DAY** – A FUNDRAISING EVENT ORGANISED BY COMIC RELIEF, WHICH HELPS PEOPLE IN NEED IN BOTH AFRICA AND THE UK.

Olly and a bunch of other brave celebrities spent **five days trekking 100 kilometres** across the VERY HOT Kaisut Desert, visiting people that they hoped to help en route. They raised an astonishing £1,300,000 for the **Comic Relief** charity.

'It was a real eye-opener for me for what's going on [in Kenya]... It was great to go over there and raise lots and lots of money and I'm hoping we can continue to do that,' said Olly afterwards.

With his football skills, Olly was an obvious choice for the **England Squad in Soccer Aid** 2012. His teammates included fellow popstars **Robbie Williams** and **Mark Owen**, comedian **John Bishop** and footballers **David Seaman** and **Teddy Sheringham,** and together they took on the Rest of the World team.

But here's the best bit. They got to play at **Old Trafford**, the home of Olly's favourite football club in the whole world – **Manchester United**.
For Olly Murs, it was a dream come true!

(AND THE ENGLAND TEAM TRIUMPHED WITH A WIN OF 3–1, WHICH MADE IT EVEN BETTER.)

Best friends **Olly Murs** and radio DJ, **Scott Mills** took part in **Let's Dance For Sport Relief** in 2012. They danced along to the **LMFAO** song **Party Rock Album** wearing enormous wigs and 1970s gear. But the big surprise came when the robot figure who'd been dancing at the back of the stage throughout their performance took off his cardboard-box hat at the end of the song to reveal that he was none other than internationally famous actor...
David Hasselhoff! (AKA **The Hoff**.)

And the **EVEN BIGGER** surprise was when they didn't win. What a shame...

[They raised a lot of money for charity though. **Hurray!**]

Did you know that Olly Murs was one of the lucky few to be immortalised in **The Beano** comic? It's true! It was all in aid of **Red Nose Day** in 2013. To celebrate the 25th anniversary of the charity, a special edition of **BeanoMax** featured cartoons of these famous names:

(Olly was in very good company.)

OLLY MURS

ONE DIRECTION

DAVID TENNANT

JESSIE J

And guess who guest-edited the comic? Top comedian, **HARRY HILL**, that's who!

OLLY MURS WAS BORN ON 14 MAY 1984, WHICH MEANS THAT ACCORDING TO THE CHINESE ZODIAC HE'S A **RAT**. (BUT NOT IN TRUE LIFE, OBVIOUSLY. HE'S REALLY A VERY NICE PERSON!)

DO you share the same sign of the chinese zodiac with your idol? Find your date of birth here to discover which sign of the chinese zodiac you are.

19 FEBRUARY 1996 – 6 FEBRUARY 1997	RAT
7 FEBRUARY 1997 – 27 JANUARY 1998	OX
28 JANUARY 1998 – 15 FEBRUARY 1999	TIGER
16 FEBRUARY 1999 – 4 FEBRUARY 2000	RABBIT
5 FEBRUARY 2000 – 23 JANUARY 2001	DRAGON

24 January 2001 – 11 February 2002	SNAKE
12 February 2002 – 31 January 2003	HORSE
1 February 2003 – 21 January 2004	GOAT
22 January 2004 – 8 February 2005	MONKEY
9 February 2005 – 28 January 2006	ROOSTER

Psst. If you know any grown-ups who are Olly Murs fans, find out when they're born. Anyone with a birthday between these dates is a RAT too...

15 February 1972 – 2 February 1973

2 February 1984 – 19 February 1985

THEY ARE POP MUSIC'S MOST
UNLIKELY DUO; CLEAN-CUT OLLY
AND THE BAD BOY OF POP, **ROBBIE
WILLIAMS**. BUT EVER SINCE THEY
FIRST MET ON **THE X FACTOR**,
THE PAIR HAVE BEEN BEST MATES.

It all began when they sang a duet
of Robbie Williams' classic ballad:
Angels. Robbie fluffed his lines,
but it was Olly who was a real
mate and got him back on track.

(What a STAR!)

Then, when Olly was named as runner-
up in **The X Factor**, it's rumoured that
Robbie texted to invite him to stay
with him in LA, perhaps to cheer him
up after the disappointing result.

(How LOVELY.)

They played on the same team for **Soccer Aid 2012**. (In real life, Robbie supports Port Vale FC, while Olly is a **Manchester United fan**, so presumably they didn't let this get in the way of a beautiful friendship.)

When Robbie decided to tour Europe in summer 2013 and was looking for an opening act, Olly Murs was the natural choice. And he was **THRILLED** to be asked.

'NOW I feel I can stand up there with Robbie, and I am the right guy to support him.'

OLLY MURS, JUST AFTER THE TOUR WAS ANNOUNCED.

Go for it, boys!

OLLY MURS HAS GOT TO BE THE SMARTEST
GUY IN SHOWBUSINESS. THERE'S NO GRUNGY
GEAR AND NO RIPPED JEANS FOR OLLY. HE'S
SO WELL-DRESSED THAT EVEN YOUR GRANNY
WOULD LIKE HIM. HERE ARE JUST A FEW OF
THE THINGS THAT YOU'LL REGULARLY SEE HIM
WEARING, BOTH ON STAGE AND OFF...

smart shirt   tailored trousers
waistcoat   posh jacket   braces
suit and tie   polo neck jumper

 # OLLY'S HATS

In the olden days, people used to say that
you were never properly dressed without a
hat. They also said that if you wanted to get
ahead, you should get a hat. Either way, Olly's
onto a winner with his **quirky headgear**.

His favourite sort of hat has got to be the
classic trilby. He wore one the ENTIRE
time he was trekking across Kenya in aid of
Comic Relief, though it looked more than a
little battered by the time he'd finished.

Definition: **trilby (noun).** a hat made from felt or tweed or straw or wool, with a narrow brim and a long dent in the crown. The term dates back to the George du Maurier novel **Trilby** (1884). When the play of the book was performed on the London stage, the actors wore this style of hat. Ever since, it's been known as a 'trilby'.

OLLY THE TV PRESENTER

HE SINGS. HE DANCES. HE WRITES CHART-TOPPING SONGS. HE CHARMS EVERYONE WITH HIS BRIGHT AND SHINY PERSONALITY. SO IT'S OBVIOUS THAT OLLY MURS SHOULD BE A TV PRESENTER TOO.

And he's actually a VERY good one.

When Olly finished singing on **THE X FACTOR** the producers couldn't bear to say goodbye to him, so when the next series came around, they asked him to come back and present the spin-off series 'XTRA FACTOR' with presenter caroline Flack.

BUT ALTHOUGH HE HAD A TERRIFIC TIME ON **XTRA FACTOR**, IN 2013 OLLY HAD TO ADMIT THAT HE COULDN'T BE A POPSTAR AND TAKE PART IN HUGE TOURS AND PRESENT A TOP TV PROGRAMME ALL AT THE SAME TIME AND HE DECIDED TO TAKE A BREAK FROM THE SHOW. 'MUSIC IS WHERE I WANT TO FOCUS AT THE MOMENT,' HE SAID. 'BUT YOU NEVER KNOW IN THIS GAME.'

So watch this space...

(Or the TV, which is where you're more likely to see him.)

Shhh...

KEEP THIS TO YOURSELF, RIGHT? THERE'S ONE
WAY THAT A GIRL CAN BE TOTALLY SURE OF
WINNING OLLY'S HEART. BUT ONCE YOU'VE
READ THIS TOP-SECRET INFORMATION, IT'S
PROBABLY BEST IF YOU PAPERCLIP THESE
PAGES SHUT SO **NO ONE ELSE** FINDS OUT.

OK, are you ready?

Olly Murs loves, loves, **LOVES** French
bulldogs. (It's understandable. They are
VERY cute. Look them up in the library or
on the Internet and you'll see just how cute
they are.) Except, Olly loves these adorable
canines so, so, **SO** much that if a girl were
to walk into his life on Valentine's Day
and give him a French bulldog puppy, he'd
marry her. (The girl, not the puppy.)

Le woof!
Le woof!

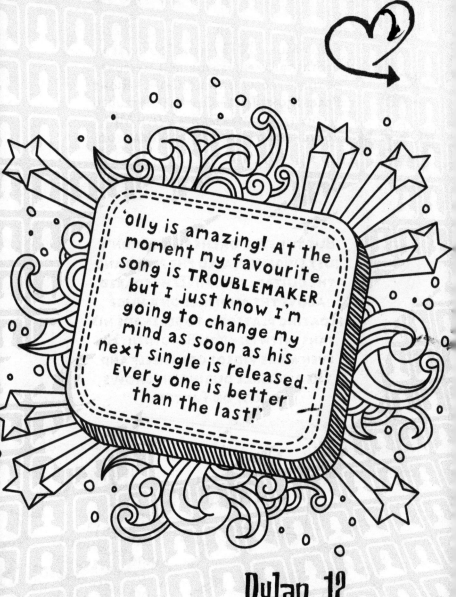

'Olly is amazing! At the moment my favourite song is **TROUBLEMAKER** but I just know I'm going to change my mind as soon as his next single is released. Every one is better than the last!'

Dylan, 12

THE 2013 ARENA TOUR

Olly Murs' 2013 Arena Tour was a total triumph. Featuring a mixture of tunes from his third album – **Right Place Right Time** – Olly also included old favourites **Dance With Me Tonight** and **Heart Skips A Beat** too.

But the star of the show didn't just sing; he played the piano and the guitar, too. AND he soared above the audience on a huge floating platform to serenade his fans with Hey You Beautiful. He even made videos of himself and the audience during his shows to post on Twitter.

Now that's multitasking.

The 2013 Arena Tour visited all of the fabulous venues listed opposite in the UK and Ireland. Where were **YOU?**

TICKET

▶ Sheffield: Motorpoint Arena
▶ Nottingham: Capital FM Arena
▶ Brighton Centre
▶ Bournemouth International Centre
▶ London: Wembley Arena
▶ Birmingham: LG Arena
▶ Liverpool: Echo Arena
▶ Glasgow: SECC
▶ Aberdeen: ECC
▶ Manchester Arena
▶ Newcastle Arena
▶ Cardiff: Motorpoint Arena
▶ London: The O2
▶ Dublin: The O2
▶ Odyssey Arena: Belfast
▶ The Embankment: Peterborough
▶ Open Air Theatre: Scarborough
▶ Middlesborough Centre Square
▶ The Marquee: Cork
▶ Dublin: Aviva Stadium
▶ Manchester: Etihad Stadium
▶ Westonbirt Arboretum: Gloucestershire
▶ Glasgow: Hampden Park
▶ London: Wembley Stadium

OUCH!

WHAT'S THE ONE THING THAT SINGERS, ACTORS AND PERFORMERS THE WORLD OVER DREAD MORE THAN ANYTHING ELSE?

Falling over on stage in front of thousands of people! And that's exactly what poor Olly did at GuilFest, a music festival in Guildford in the UK, in 2012.

It happened while he was singing the classic Stevie Wonder hit, **Signed, Sealed, Delivered, I'm Yours**. Olly strolled towards a set of steps (stage left), went down two steps and...

PLUNGED OUT OF SIGHT!

But as soon as he'd slid right to the bottom, Olly shouted into his mic, **'I'm all right. It's all right.'** And carried right on singing.

What a pro!

by @Ollyofficial

(To find out what happened between Olly and JLS, go to page 30-31...)

STILL RECOVERING, STILL SHAKING & STILL SHOCKED!! @JLSOFFICIAL YOU GOT ME PROPER TODAY!!

LOVE HAVING BIZARRE DREAMS... MAKES ME NOT WANT TO GET UP!!

1ST TIME IN BRUSSELS TODAY!! ME LIKEY WHAT I SEE ALREADY ALREADY!! BONJOUR!!

MY DRESSING ROOM IS SO HOT... THAT I'M CURRENTLY CUDDLING UP TO THE FRIDGE! #MELTING

OLLY MURS IS THE FIRST PERSON EVER TO TAKE PART IN THE GAME SHOW **DEAL OR NO DEAL** TWICE. HE FIRST APPEARED ON **DEAL OR NO DEAL** IN 2007, BEFORE HE WAS FAMOUS. HE CAME AWAY WITH JUST A £10 PRIZE, WHICH PROBABLY WASN'T EVEN ENOUGH TO PAY HIS TRAVEL EXPENSES.

The next time Olly appeared on **Deal or no Deal**, it was for a celebrity special. It was all to play for. This time, surely he would win a **HUGE** amount of money for Brainwave – the children's charity he'd chosen to support.

But he won just 50p.

He's sticking to the day job.

OLLY MURS IS ONE OF THOSE RARE POPSTARS WHO DOESN'T JUST SING THE SONGS THAT OTHER SONGWRITERS PEN FOR HIM – HE WRITES THEM HIMSELF TOO. BUT THE AMAZING THING IS THAT HE DIDN'T EVEN **KNOW** THAT HE COULD WRITE SONGS BEFORE HE WAS ASKED TO HAVE A GO.

After working together with established pros, Olly appears on the writing credits of the chart-topping **Please Don't Let Me Go**, **Dance With Me Tonight** and **Troublemaker**, a platinum-selling monster of a hit.

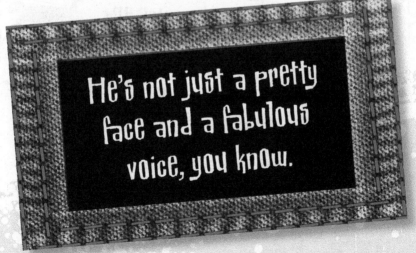

He's not just a pretty face and a fabulous voice, you know.

SO FAR, HE'S HEADLINED TWO FABULOUS TOURS OF HIS OWN – AND THERE ARE SURE TO BE MANY MORE – BUT OLLY DOESN'T MIND SUPPORTING HIS POP FRIENDS WITH THEIR TOURS, TOO...

In the summer of 2012, Olly Murs toured America with a boy band that you just may have heard of (unless you've been living on the Moon for the last five years!) Who are they? **ONE DIRECTION**, of course! For six fabulous weeks, Olly opened for One D, performing sell-out shows in Canada and the USA.

> 'Touring with One Direction is going to be nuts!' Olly said beforehand.
>
> **it was.**

So how could Olly Murs top that? What could be **EVEN BETTER** than touring with the biggest boy band of the 21st century...? Touring with a member of one of the biggest boy bands of the 20th century, that's what.

WHEN **ROBBIE WILLIAMS** WAS LOOKING
FOR A SPECIAL GUEST FOR HIS EUROPEAN
STADIUM TOUR 2013 – HE LOOKED NO
FURTHER THAN HIS BEST MATE, OLLY.

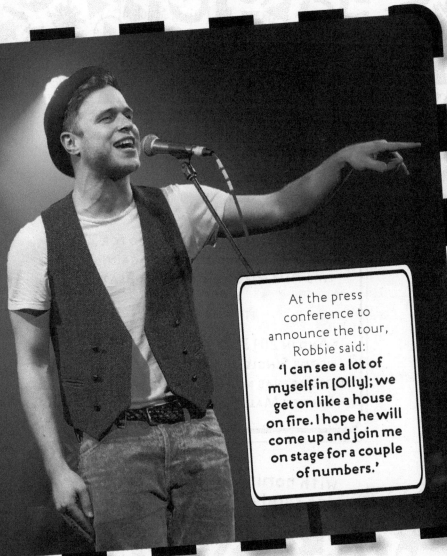

At the press
conference to
announce the tour,
Robbie said:
**'I can see a lot of
myself in [Olly]; we
get on like a house
on fire. I hope he will
come up and join me
on stage for a couple
of numbers.'**

IN 2011, OLLY MURS WON THE BEST BRITISH ALBUM AT THE RADIO 1 TEEN AWARDS.

 He's also racked up a stack of nominations at the Brit Awards — the biggest pop music awards in the UK.

- IN 2011, **PLEASE DON'T LET ME GO** WAS NOMINATED FOR THE BRITISH SINGLE AWARD.

- IN 2012, HE WAS NOMINATED FOR THE BRITISH SINGLE AWARD AGAIN, THIS TIME FOR **HEART SKIPS A BEAT**.

- AND IN 2013, **TROUBLEMAKER** WAS UP FOR SINGLE OF THE YEAR AND OLLY HIMSELF WAS NOMINATED FOR THE BEST BRITISH MALE SOLO ARTIST AWARD.

 with nominations like these, it's surely only a matter of time before olly wins  **BIG.**

People need
to lose this whole,
like, he's-from-THE-X-
FACTOR stigma because it's
been a while and he's one of the
only people from THE X FACTOR
to have a career. He works hard.
He doesn't think he's the best;
he doesn't think he's the worst.
He's a humble dude and needs to
be recognised in some way...
someone needs to tip their
hat and go,

'Well done!'

ED SHEERAN,
SPEAKING ON
CAPITAL FM

In 2013, Olly Murs starred in one of the last-ever episodes of the long-running US teen drama **90210**. The acting wasn't that tricky – he made a cameo appearance, as **HIMSELF!** But Olly also got the chance to do what he's best known for – singing. In the show, he sang **TROUBLEMAKER** and **RIGHT PLACE RIGHT TIME** on set.

If you managed to catch this episode on TV, what did you think of Olly's acting debut? Is he going to be as successful at acting as he already is at being a pop star...?

'It was good to be a part of [90210] and I get to play myself. They scripted a performance into the show and that's kind of what my role is – it's nothing amazing. I'm definitely not going to win an Emmy for it! It's a great show for me to be a part of. Acting is something I would love to do in the future, but obviously I'm focussed on music at the moment.'

by
Olly Murs

'I love, love, LOVE Olly Murs. It's not just because he's a good singer though. I love how his music isn't just pop, but has real meaning to it'.

Josie, 12

In January 2013, Olly was named as an official ambassador for the **Football Association (FA)**. This would be an amazing achievement at any time, but it was announced on the actual 150th anniversary of the FA, which makes it an even bigger deal and **a huge honour**!

'I'm delighted to be an official ambassador for the Football Association for its 150th anniversary year,' said Olly after the announcement. 'I'm a huge football fan and will be involved in FA events and initiatives over the course of this year. In particular, I want to help to showcase the amazing work the FA does at the grass roots level of the game.'

Well done, Olly.

So you think you know Olly Murs'
full name? But do you? All of
it? Sure about that? Find Olly's
actual names in the right order
from the list below...

OLLY STANLEY MURS

★★★★★

OLIVER STANFORD MURS

★★★★★

OLIVER STANLEY MURS

★★★★★

OLIVER HARDY MURS

★★★★★

STANLEY OLIVER MURS

★★★★★

 All answers on
pages 90-93

ARMY OF TWO
is a song that is
actually about the fans...
It could also be about a
relationship with someone,
but we wrote it with the fans
in mind. We're like an army who
work together to keep pushing
forward. I want to grow
with my fans like Robbie
[Williams] did.

Olly Murs

'WHEN YOU SEE FAME, FAMOUS PEOPLE, ON THE TELLY AND THAT, IT ALL LOOKS SO EASY... RED CARPETS, FALLING OUT OF CLUBS, GIRLS. BUT IN REALITY, IT'S HARD WORK, RELENTLESS HARD WORK, DAY AND NIGHT. TO GET ANYWHERE IN THIS INDUSTRY, YOU NEED TO BE A WORKAHOLIC. THAT'S WHAT THREE YEARS IN THIS BUSINESS HAS TAUGHT ME.'

Olly Murs

TOP TWEETS

by @ollyofficial

Wow... Looooooooooong day!! Rehearsals going well... Stage is cool... But scary if ya know what I mean!! ;)

LOVE BOURNEMOUTH... SPECIALLY STRAIGHT AFTER BRIGHTON... OH I DO LIKE TO BE BESIDE THE SEASIDE OH I DO LIKE TO BE BESIDE THE SEA!

Tonight I swear was a dream But I did get a picture to prove so it must be real! Finally met Mila Kunis I was SO NOT cool about it!

AWWW THAT LITTLE GIRL GIVING ME THE FLOWERS AFTER 'ONE OF THESE DAYS' WAS VERY SCH-WEET!!x

SPOT THE ALBUM!

SO YOU KNOW OLLY MURS' SONGS BACK TO FRONT? EXCELLENT. BUT CAN YOU IDENTIFY WHICH ALBUM EACH OF THE FOLLOWING LESSER-KNOWN TRACKS COME FROM ...? GRAB A PEN AND PAPER AND FIND OUT!

1. A Million More Years

a. Olly Murs

b. In Case You Didn't Know

c. Right Place Right Time

2. Head to Toe

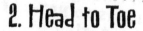

a. Olly Murs

b. In Case You Didn't Know

c. Right Place Right Time

3. I'm OK

a. Olly Murs

b. In Case You Didn't Know

c. Right Place Right Time

4. Busy

a. Olly Murs

b. In Case You Didn't Know

c. Right Place Right Time

There's more

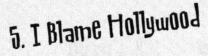

5. I Blame Hollywood

a. Olly Murs

b. In Case You Didn't Know

c. Right Place Right Time

6. Just Smile

a. Olly Murs

b. In Case You Didn't Know

c. Right Place Right Time

All answers on pages 90-93

WOW!

OLLY MURS MIGHT HAVE PERFORMED
WITH SOME OF THE BIGGEST NAMES IN
THE MUSIC BUSINESS, BUT ON
THE X FACTOR LIVE HE SANG WITH
A **HOLLYWOOD LEGEND**...

>>> yes, REALLY. <<<

The legendary Muppets provided star-studded accompaniment to DANCE WITH ME TONIGHT with Miss Piggy on backing vocals and Fozzy Bear on double bass. Olly finished off the performance by kissing Miss Piggy's trotter!

Awww.

How well do **YOU** know Olly Murs? Grab a pen and paper and try your luck with this totally tricky trivia quiz to find out...

1. Which instruments does Olly Murs play...?

The harp and the trombone
The piano and the glockenspiel
The piano and the guitar
The harp and the harpsichord

2. Which of these Hollywood stars has Olly Murs sung with...?

Johnny Depp
The Muppets
Mila Kunis
Cate Blanchett

3. WHICH OF THESE SPORTS IS OLLY MURS REALLY GOOD AT...?

Snowboarding
Skydiving
Hurdling
Playing football

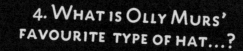

4. WHAT IS OLLY MURS' FAVOURITE TYPE OF HAT...?

Stetson
Bowler
Trilby
Woolly

5. WHO WAS OLLY MURS' CO-PRESENTER ON XTRA FACTOR...?

Tess Daly
Caroline Flack
Roberta Flack
Dannii Minogue

6. WHICH POPSTAR WAS OLLY MURS' INSPIRATION...?

Michael Jackson
Justin Timberlake
Bruno Mars
Taylor Swift

7. WHICH OF THESE VENUES DID OLLY MURS NOT VISIT ON HIS 2013 ARENA TOUR...?

Liverpool: Echo Arena
Sydney, Aus: ANZ Stadium
London: The O2
Glasgow: Hampden Park

8. WHO INVITED OLLY MURS TO GO AND STAY WITH HIM AFTER THE X FACTOR FINAL...?

Gary Barlow
Mark Owen
Howard Donald
Jason Orange
Robbie Williams

All answers on pages 90-93

THE BIG QUIZ

So, you've read the book and soaked up the facts. Do you know your idol now? Check out this mega-quiz to find out if you're a true Olly Murs fan. There are three parts to test your knowledge to the max.

1. What is Olly Murs' sister called?

2. Which 1884 novel by George du Maurier is the trilby hat named after?

3. How many times did Olly audition for The X Factor?

4. How tall is he?

5. When is his birthday?

6. Which football team does he support?

7. What job did he do before he was famous?

8. What are the titles of his first three albums?

9. Who wrote and sang the classic hit Superstition that Olly sang on The X Factor?

10. What colour are his eyes?

Were your answers FAN-tastic?

If you're up for a challenge, turn over the page to continue with **THE BIG QUIZ**. But beware – it's for true fans only...

11. WHICH MEMBER OF JLS DID HE FIRE OUT OF A CANNON?

12. WHAT IS HIS FAVOURITE COLOUR?

13. IS OLLY AN OLDER OR A YOUNGER TWIN?

14. ON WHICH HOLLYWOOD STAR DOES HE HAVE A CRUSH?

15. WHAT'S THE WEIRDEST THING HE HAS EVER SIGNED?

16. WHAT SORT OF DANCING IS HE FAMOUS FOR?

17. WHICH SIGN OF THE CHINESE ZODIAC IS HE?

18. IS HE A FAN OF KARAOKE MACHINES?

19. WHERE IS HIS DAD'S FAMILY ORIGINALLY FROM?

20. WHO OFFERED HIM A RECORD DEAL?

21. Is his favourite pudding cheesecake or ice cream?

★★★★★

22. What's his favourite Michael Jackson song?

★★★★★

23. If he could take one thing to a desert island, what would it be?

★★★★★

24. What's the most gourmet meal he can cook?

★★★★★

25. Which knee did he injure to end his football career?

26. Name one person who shares a birthday with Olly.

★★★★★

27. What smelly stuff does he love?

★★★★★

28. Which English county does he come from?

★★★★★

29. What's the name of his autobiography?

★★★★★

30. What's his middle name?

All answers on pages 90-93
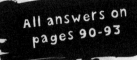

>>> Singles <<<

PLEASE DON'T LET ME GO
29 AUGUST 2010

THINKING OF ME
19 NOVEMBER 2010

HEART ON MY SLEEVE
6 MARCH 2011

BUSY
(WITH **THE X FACTOR** FINALISTS 2011)
27 MAY 2011

HEART SKIPS A BEAT
(FEATURING RIZZLE KICKS)
19 AUGUST 2011

DANCE WITH ME TONIGHT
18 NOVEMBER 2011

OH MY GOODNESS
1 APRIL 2012

TROUBLEMAKER
(FEATURING FLO RIDA)
8 OCTOBER 2012

ARMY OF TWO
10 MARCH 2013

⟩⟩⟩ Albums ⟨⟨⟨

OLLY MURS
29 NOVEMBER 2010

CHANGE IS GONNA COME

PLEASE DON'T LET ME GO

THINKING OF ME

BUSY

I BLAME HOLLYWOOD

ASK ME TO STAY

HEART ON MY SLEEVE

HOLD ON

ACCIDENTAL

LOVE SHINE DOWN

DON'T SAY GOODBYE

A MILLION MORE YEARS

>>> Albums <<<

IN CASE YOU DIDN'T KNOW
25 NOVEMBER 2011

HEART SKIPS A BEAT
(FEATURING RIZZLE KICKS)

OH MY GOODNESS

DANCE WITH ME TONIGHT

I'VE TRIED EVERYTHING

THIS SONG IS ABOUT YOU

IN CASE YOU DIDN'T KNOW

TELL THE WORLD

I'M OK

JUST SMILE

ON MY CLOUD

I DON'T LOVE YOU TOO

ANYWHERE ELSE

I NEED YOU NOW

>>> Albums <<<

Right Place Right Time
26 November 2012

Army Of Two

Troublemaker
(featuring Flo Rida)

Loud and Clear

Dear Darlin'

Right Place Right Time

Hand On Heart

Hey You Beautiful

Head To Toe

Personal

What A Buzz

Cry Your Heart Out

One Of These Days

Dear Darlin' – the third single Olly released from his third album, **Right Place Right Time** – was inspired by none other than **Eminem**. In the über-rapper's track entitled **Stan** (released in 2000), the lyrics are written as if they are letters being read aloud. So that's what Olly did when he was penning **Dear Darlin'** with Ed Drewett and Jim Eliot. He wrote a letter to a long-lost love.

Awww.

WHAT'S NEXT FOR OLLY MURS?

Olly Murs has already conquered the **UK** charts. He has two solo tours **AND** tours with **One Direction** and **Robbie Williams** under his belt. So where does he go from here?

The USA, of course!

Cracking the USA is a tough thing for a UK artist to achieve, but if anyone can do it, Olly can. And he's already toured there with **One Direction**, so he has a head start.

will he do it?

Watch this USA-shaped space.

Pages 20-21
WHICH OF THESE TRACKS HASN'T OLLY RELEASED?

OLIVER'S ARMY
DON'T LEAVE ME THIS WAY
DANCING QUEEN
HEART OF GLASS
TROUBLE
DO YOU THINK OF ME

Pages 28-29
MIX AND MATCH

1. PLEASE DON'T LET ME GO
2. HEART SKIPS A BEAT
3. DANCE WITH ME TONIGHT
4. TROUBLEMAKER
5. ARMY OF TWO
6. THINKING OF ME

ALBUMS
OLLY MURS:
PLEASE DON'T LET ME GO,
THINKING OF ME
IN CASE YOU DIDN'T KNOW:
HEART SKIPS A BEAT,
DANCE WITH ME TONIGHT

RIGHT PLACE RIGHT TIME:
TROUBLEMAKER,
ARMY OF TWO

Page 66
STUCK IN THE MIDDLE
OLIVER STANLEY MURS

Pages 70-72
SPOT THE ALBUM
1. A) OLLY MURS
2. C) RIGHT PLACE RIGHT TIME
3. B) IN CASE YOU DIDN'T KNOW
4. A) OLLY MURS
5. A) OLLY MURS
6. B) IN CASE YOU DIDN'T KNOW

Pages 74-77
TOP TRIVIA QUIZ
1. THE PIANO AND THE GUITAR
2. THE MUPPETS
3. PLAYING FOOTBALL
4. TRILBY
5. CAROLINE FLACK
6. MICHAEL JACKSON
7. ANZ STADIUM, SYDNEY, AUSTRALIA
8. ROBBIE WILLIAMS

QUIZ ANSWERS

Pages 78-83
THE BIG QUIZ

1. FAY

2. TRILBY

3. THREE TIMES

4. HE'S 175 CM OR 5 FEET 9 INCHES TALL

5. 14 MAY

6. MANCHESTER UNITED

7. HE WORKED IN TELESALES IN A CALL CENTRE

8. OLLY MURS, IN CASE YOU DIDN'T KNOW AND RIGHT PLACE RIGHT TIME

9. STEVIE WONDER

10. ORANGE...ONLY JOKING! BROWN

11. AHA! THIS IS A TRICK QUESTION. HE ACTUALLY FIRED A STUNTMAN OUT OF A CANNON. BUT HE **THOUGHT** THAT THE HUMAN CANNONBALL WAS ASTON MERRYGOLD, SO YOU SCORE HALF A POINT IF THAT WAS YOUR ANSWER!

12. BLUE

13. OLDER

14. MILA KUNIS

QUIZ ANSWERS

15. A FAN
16. ROBOTIC
17. RAT
18. YES!
19. LATVIA
20. SIMON COWELL
21. HE LIKES THEM **BOTH**
22. BILLIE JEAN
23. A GADGET ON WHICH TO PLAY HIS FAVOURITE MUSIC.
24. BEANS ON TOAST WITH CHEESE ON TOP.
25. LEFT
26. HIS BROTHER BEN OR MARK ZUCKERBERG OR MIRANDA COSGROVE OR CATE BLANCHETT OR GEORGE LUCAS.
27. COLOGNE
28. ESSEX
29. HAPPY DAYS
30. STANLEY

INDEX

Congratulations!

Now you really, truly **KNOW** your idol (probably better than his own mum). But what about your **OTHER** idols, like **One Direction**, **Justin Bieber**, **Katy Perry**, **Robert Pattinson** and **James Arthur?**

WHAT ABOUT THEM...?

DON'T PANIC.

Simply check out the other titles in the series and become an

EVEN BIGGER FAN.

Want to Know Your Idol?

TOTALLY AWESOME TITLES IN THE SERIES:

9780750279321

9780750279338

9780750279307

9780750279314

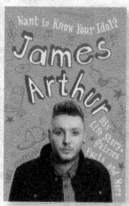

9780750278386

9780750278362

WHY NOT COLLECT THEM ALL?